Psalms

Sing to the Savior

Angela Lee

Endorsements

"Angela insightfully brings the ancient text of Psalms into this day and age; the joys and the sorrows of daily life. She offers a gospel-saturated look at some of the most beloved Biblical books to reveal Jesus to us in the Old Testament. It's an honor to endorse her study on the Psalms and I encourage you to buy a copy of your own — you'll be blessed."
– Madeline Wilkins, Writer and Mom of 3.

"*Psalms: Sing to the Savior* is a beautifully written study that draws its readers into a closer knowledge of God's Word. Not only does Angela teach the Word clearly, but she also gently nudges readers to inspect their own hearts and grow in their obedience and relationship with Christ by seeing Him in the Psalms."
- Kelly Cooper, Training Facilitator, Reaching & Teaching International Ministries

Table of Contents

A Plan for This Study

This study is based on the Observation, Interpretation, and Application method of Bible study. The questions and commentary move you through these steps:

Observation: What does the text say?
Read the entire text for comprehension.
Read again and consider: Who was this written to? What is happening in the passage? When and where did this take place? Why did the author write this?
Mark any keywords, repeated phrases, or ideas.
Notice any lists, contrasts, comparisons, or types of imagery used.

Interpretation: What does the text mean?
Consult different translations.
Look up cross-references.
What would the original hearers have thought?
How does this passage fit into the greater story of the Bible? (Creation-Fall-Redemption-New Creation)
Paraphrase: Rewrite the text in your own words.
Consult reliable commentaries.

Application: How do I apply it to my life?
What does this passage tell us about God?
What does this passage tell you about your sin and your need for a Savior?
Is there a command to obey? A promise to claim?
How might this truth transform my life and perspective today?

Each lesson consists of Observation and Interpretation questions, devotional commentary and teaching, Application questions, and an invitation to journal or pray the psalm in your own words.

An additional way to worship using Psalms is memorization. To guide you in this, there is a plan within the study to assist you in memorizing Psalm 1.

Psalms

Introduction
Background and Purpose of the Psalms

Observation and Interpretation

1. David wrote most of the psalms we cover in this study. Read **1 Samuel 13:13-14** (verse 14 refers to David as God's choice) and **1 Samuel 16:7-13** and consider: what do you learn about David's life and walk with God?

¹³ And Samuel said to Saul, "You have done foolishly. You have not kept the command of the Lord your God, with which he commanded you. For then the Lord would have established your kingdom over Israel forever. ¹⁴ But now your kingdom shall not continue. The Lord has sought out a man after his own heart, and the Lord has commanded him to be prince over his people, because you have not kept what the Lord commanded you."

7 But the Lord said to Samuel, "Do not look on his appearance or on the height of his stature, because I have rejected him. For the Lord sees not as man sees: man looks on the outward appearance, but the Lord looks on the heart." 8 Then Jesse called Abinadab and made him pass before Samuel. And he said, "Neither has the Lord chosen this one." 9 Then Jesse made Shammah pass by. And he said, "Neither has the Lord chosen this one." 10 And Jesse made seven of his sons pass before Samuel. And Samuel said to Jesse, "The Lord has not chosen these." 11 Then Samuel said to Jesse, "Are all your sons here?" And he said, "There remains yet the youngest,[a] but behold, he is keeping the sheep." And Samuel said to Jesse, "Send and get him, for we will not sit down till he comes here." 12 And he sent and brought him in. Now he was ruddy and had beautiful eyes and was handsome. And the Lord said, "Arise, anoint him, for this is he." 13 Then Samuel took the horn of oil and anointed him in the midst of his brothers. And the Spirit of the Lord rushed upon David from that day forward. And Samuel rose up and went to Ramah.

2. How might our knowledge of David's life inform us as we read the Psalms?

Psalms 1 and 2 serve as an introduction to the Psalter; they help us understand the purpose of the five books of Psalms. **Read Psalms 1 and 2 and consider the following questions.**

Psalm 1

1 Blessed is the man
 who walks not in the counsel of the wicked,
nor stands in the way of sinners,
 nor sits in the seat of scoffers;
2 but his delight is in the law[b] of the Lord,
 and on his law he meditates day and night.
3 He is like a tree
 planted by streams of water
that yields its fruit in its season,
 and its leaf does not wither.
In all that he does, he prospers.
4 The wicked are not so,
 but are like chaff that the wind drives away.
5 Therefore the wicked will not stand in the judgment,
 nor sinners in the congregation of the righteous;
6 for the Lord knows the way of the righteous,
 but the way of the wicked will perish.

Psalm 2

1 Why do the nations rage
 and the peoples plot in vain?
2 The kings of the earth set themselves,
 and the rulers take counsel together,
 against the Lord and against his Anointed, saying,
3 "Let us burst their bonds apart
 and cast away their cords from us."
4 He who sits in the heavens laughs;
 the Lord holds them in derision.

[5] Then he will speak to them in his wrath,
  and terrify them in his fury, saying,
[6] "As for me, I have set my King
  on Zion, my holy hill."
[7] I will tell of the decree:
The Lord said to me, "You are my Son;
  today I have begotten you.
[8] Ask of me, and I will make the nations your heritage,
  and the ends of the earth your possession.
[9] You shall break them with a rod of iron
  and dash them in pieces like a potter's vessel."
[10] Now therefore, O kings, be wise;
  be warned, O rulers of the earth.
[11] Serve the Lord with fear,
  and rejoice with trembling.
[12] Kiss the Son,
  lest he be angry, and you perish in the way,
  for his wrath is quickly kindled.
Blessed are all who take refuge in him.

1. From Psalm 1, underline the characteristics and actions of the righteous.

2. What are some things that the righteous do **not** do?

3. Think about the life of Jesus. List some ways Jesus fulfilled the righteous life described in Psalm 1.

4. Psalm 2 was a coronation song for the kings of Israel. But there is language hinting that this psalm might have another layer of meaning. What verses or phrases in Psalm 2 point us to not only an Israelite king but a future king of all nations?

5. Psalm 2 is quoted in **Acts 4:24-30, 13:32-34, Revelation 2:26-27**, and many other parts of the New Testament. Considering these verses, describe how Jesus Christ fulfills Psalm 2.

Acts 4:24-30

24 And when they heard it, they lifted their voices together to God and said, "Sovereign Lord, who made the heaven and the earth and the sea and everything in them, 25 who through the mouth of our father David, your servant,[d] said by the Holy Spirit,

"'Why did the Gentiles rage,
   and the peoples plot in vain?
26 The kings of the earth set themselves,
   and the rulers were gathered together,
   against the Lord and against his Anointed' —

27 for truly in this city there were gathered together against your holy servant Jesus, whom you anointed, both Herod and Pontius Pilate, along with the Gentiles and the peoples of Israel, 28 to do whatever your hand and your plan had predestined to take place. 29 And now, Lord, look upon their threats and grant to your servants to continue to speak your word with all boldness, 30 while you stretch out your hand to heal, and signs and wonders are performed through the name of your holy servant Jesus."

Acts 13:32-34

[32] And we bring you the good news that what God promised to the fathers, [33] this he has fulfilled to us their children by raising Jesus, as also it is written in the second Psalm,

"'You are my Son,
today I have begotten you.'

[34] And as for the fact that he raised him from the dead, no more to return to corruption, he has spoken in this way,

Revelation 2:26-27

[26] The one who conquers and who keeps my works until the end, to him I will give authority over the nations, [27] and he will rule them with a rod of iron, as when earthen pots are broken in pieces, even as I myself have received authority from my Father.

6. Psalm 2:10-12 states what our response should be to the reality of the ruling Messiah in Psalm 2. Describe this response in your own words.

Commentary and Teaching

Who wrote the Psalms?

David is the most common writer of the Psalms (75 psalms), then the Sons of Korah (11 psalms), Asaph (12 psalms), Solomon (2 psalms), and Moses (1 psalm). Many psalms do not have a writer attributed to them.

Where do the Psalms fit within the context of the whole Bible?

God created us to praise and worship Him. He made men and women in His image and likeness (Genesis 1:26-28), and they were to bring Him glory through their adoration of Him. After the fall, sin separated humanity from God (Genesis 3). Their perspective of God and their ability to know and praise Him was distorted, but God promised to send His people a Messiah—a Savior to restore them to perfect and pure worship. He chose Abraham to be a part of that plan. God made a covenant with him to bless his family, make them a nation, and provide a place for them (Genesis 12). Abraham's family became the Hebrew nation of Israel. Through many trials and wanderings, including enslavement in Egypt (Exodus 1), God was faithful to pursue Israel. The Israelites' sinful state made it so they couldn't be in God's presence without mediators. So, through Moses, the law and sacrificial system were put in place, and the tabernacle was built—where God dwelled amongst His people (Exodus 19-31).

Later in Israel's history, King David dreamed of a temple; it would be a house where God's tabernacle might dwell, God's word would be spoken, and others would come to **worship Him through prayer and song** (2 Samuel 7). God used David's son Solomon to build this temple, and a second was built about 500 years later under the leadership of Ezra.

As the people continued to wait for God's rescue, they wavered and stumbled into sin, suffered under wicked kings, and even experienced exile. The sinful hearts and deep, painful trials of God's people seemed to make worship confusing. What were they to say to God when they didn't understand their circumstances? How were they to talk to God as they grieved? How were they to thank and praise Him as they waited for a Messiah? And how would all of this be spoken in a way that was grounded in God's truth? Worship leaders like David and Asaph were appointed to lead God's people in song in the temple. Through their own seasons of thanksgiving and affliction, and inspired by the Holy Spirit, these songwriters wrote prayers, poems, and songs of many genres that aided God's people in their praise.

These prayers, poems, and songs were recorded, collected, and organized into the book of Psalms. The Psalms, a title meaning the "book of praises," gave God's people truthful words for their lament, wisdom for their waiting and trials, and heart songs for their thanksgiving and praise. **God gave them a language of prayer and worship** so that they might intimately know Him while they waited for their Messiah, Jesus Christ, who would dwell "tabernacling" among them (John 1:14) as the fulfillment of every prayer and song. God's people continue to use the Psalms as they behold Jesus Christ and trust that He will one day come again to restore them to full and perfect worship (Revelation 21-22).

What kind of literature are the Psalms?

The Psalms are a collection of poems and prayers. Many were set to song and used in corporate worship at the temple. When reading and interpreting psalms, consider the use of imagery in poetry: image, metaphor, simile, personification, and hyperbole.

The Psalms are written in the verse form of parallelism, which is: "the art of saying something twice with the difference added in the second colon" (Futato, 2002, p. 36).

Example: Psalm 96:1
"Sing to the Lord a new song;
Sing to the Lord, all the earth. "

In this verse, the first line expresses what is being sung to the Lord, and the second verse specifies the person doing the singing.

There are many themes in the Psalms. The ones covered in this study will be psalms of **lament, thanksgiving, wisdom, and praise.**

Note: There are many more components involved in Hebrew poetry. The above listed are just a few that are helpful for study.

When were the Psalms written?

The individual psalms come from several different periods in Israel's history, from the time of Moses (15th or 13th century B.C) to the time of David and Solomon (10th Century B.C) (ESV Study Bible).

How is the book of Psalms organized?

These poems are organized into five books, with Psalms 1 and 2 arranged as an introduction. There are five books of Psalms, and each book ends with a doxology – or a call to praise God (for example, Book 1 ends with a doxology in Psalm 41:13). The exact structure of the books isn't stated, and while there are many theories and ideas, the organization method is not widely agreed upon. The book of Psalms is most simply a songbook for the people of God.

What is the purpose of the Psalms?

"A key insight into the Book of Psalms is found in the ancient Hebrew title. The message found in the ancient title can be summarized in one word: praise. We could call the book the Book of Praises" Mark D. Futato (2002, p. 4).

The Psalter serves as a songbook for the worshiping people of God, and these psalms guide us in our approach to worship, prayer, and praise. Some psalms were written as private poems or prayers that were later used in worship; others were written for specific festivals or celebrations. In addition to being used for private and corporate worship, they provide instructions on how to live a blessed, holy, and worshipful life in God's Kingdom.

When we read these songs and prayers, they give us words to express our own emotions and longings to God. We can learn from the models of the inspired writers, who sought the Lord in their seasons of trial, thanksgiving, and praise. The Psalms model conversation and worship that are direct, intense, emotional, intimate, and deeply honest. When our emotions and circumstances overwhelm us and we are unsure of how to bring them before the Lord, the Psalms can be a guide for us — they help us process these feelings in a way that is grounded in God's word.

The Psalms were one of God's gracious gifts to Israel as they sojourned and learned how to worship Him in a broken world. They also serve as a doctrinal treasure. As writers like Paul wrote and spoke to spread the knowledge of God, he quoted the Psalms more than any other Old Testament book. These prayers tell us precious details about the character and nature of God, such as His omniscience, His unparalleled power over nature, and His infinite sovereignty; the Psalms are imperative in forming our knowledge of God's attributes.

Themes We Will Focus On

In this study, we will approach the Psalms by studying four different genres of Psalms. Each lesson will focus on a particular psalm and how it points to Jesus.

Psalms of Lament

How do we pray when we don't see evidence of blessing in our lives, when we feel we are drowning in trial and pain, or when we are overwhelmed with our sin? Psalms of Lament give us honest, bold language for how to lay difficult situations before the Lord and ask for help. Laments are offered amid deep sorrow and serve as scripts to lead us to a deep trust in our Savior.

Psalms of Thanksgiving

These psalms can guide us in thanking God for answered prayer and for His blessing and character toward us as they grant us a heart posture of gratitude.

Psalms of Wisdom

These are psalms that take the themes from wisdom books (Job, Proverbs, Ecclesiastes, Song of Solomon) and put them to songs. They show us how to ask God for His wisdom when we are in humbling or perplexing circumstances.

Psalms of Praise

The aim of these hymns is to call people to praise God. They include reminders of His salvation, His attributes, His sovereignty and kingship, and His work in creation.

How do the Psalms of Lament, Thanksgiving, Wisdom, and Praise point us to Christ?

After His resurrection, Jesus instructed how we are to interpret books like the Psalms.

"Then he said to them, 'These are my words that I spoke to you while I was still with you, that everything written about me in the Law of Moses and the Prophets and the Psalms must be fulfilled." Then he opened their minds to understand the Scriptures and said to them, 'Thus it is written, that the Christ should suffer and on the third day rise from the dead, and that repentance for the forgiveness of sins should be proclaimed in his name to all nations, beginning from Jerusalem.'" (Luke 24:44-47)

Every psalm finds its fulfillment and answer in Jesus Christ. Jesus is the answer to the psalmist's *laments* as he cries for rescue, redemption, and forgiveness (Psalms 13, 51). As we wrestle with God and ask for His *wisdom*, we learn that the perfect *wisdom* of God is hidden in Christ (Colossians 2:3) (Psalms 131, 73). And at the cross, Jesus secures the blessings and salvation that we *thank* and *praise* God for (Psalms 32, 30, 19, 103).

Psalms 1 and 2

As they introduce the Psalms, Psalm 1 tells us to read the Psalms as a guide to living a Christ-like, worship-filled life, and Psalm 2 shows us to read the Psalms in light of this truth: Jesus reigns. Throughout the life of Christ, He righteously and perfectly worshiped God through lament, thanksgiving, wisdom, and praise as He meditated on the word (Psalm 1). When the psalmists cry out for the Messiah to deliver us from sin and usher in a new heaven and earth, our hope is in Christ and His return (Psalm 2). For the people of Israel, this meant meditating on scripture while hoping in the coming Messiah, and trusting that God had set His king on the throne. For the church today, it means the Psalms instruct us to meditate on the word while trusting in the finished work and expected return of our Messiah and Lord, Jesus Christ.

"The first (psalm) shows us the character and lot of the righteous; and the next teaches us that the psalms are Messianic, and speak of Christ the Messiah — the Prince who will reign from the river unto the ends of the earth" -Charles Spurgeon (1993, p. 8).

We sing and pray these psalms of lament, thanksgiving, wisdom, and praise with this in mind: meditate on the word and live a righteous life while you take refuge in Jesus; trust that He is on the throne and He is coming soon.

Application and Reflection

1. How should the context and background of the Psalms help us as we study and apply them?

2. What are your thoughts about the fact that in order to help His people wait for the Messiah, God gave them songs to sing?

3. How has God moved in your heart through songs?

4. As you study the Psalms, what is something you want to learn or grow in regarding your communication with God?

Lament

Psalm 13

Observation and Interpretation

Read Psalm 13 and consider the following questions.

¹ How long, O Lord? Will you forget me forever?
  How long will you hide your face from me?
² How long must I take counsel in my soul
  and have sorrow in my heart all the day?
How long shall my enemy be exalted over me?
³ Consider and answer me, O Lord my God;
  light up my eyes, lest I sleep the sleep of death,
⁴ lest my enemy say, "I have prevailed over him,"
  lest my foes rejoice because I am shaken.
⁵ But I have trusted in your steadfast love;
  my heart shall rejoice in your salvation.
⁶ I will sing to the Lord,
  because he has dealt bountifully with me.

1. What is David's complaint in verses 1-2?

2. What does David's language tell us about his relationship with God?

3. Describe David's request in verses 3-4.

4. In verses 5-6, David makes a transition and puts his hope in God. Hannah makes a similar transition at the end of her prayer in **1 Samuel 1:12-18**. Read these passages and reflect: what helped them get to this place of peace?

[12] As she continued praying before the Lord, Eli observed her mouth.[13] Hannah was speaking in her heart; only her lips moved, and her voice was not heard. Therefore Eli took her to be a drunken woman.[14] And Eli said to her, "How long will you go on being drunk? Put your wine away from you." [15] But Hannah answered, "No, my lord, I am a woman troubled in spirit. I have drunk neither wine nor strong drink, but I have been pouring out my soul before the Lord. [16] Do not regard your servant as a worthless woman, for all along I have been speaking out of my great anxiety and vexation." [17] Then Eli answered, "Go in peace, and the God of Israel grant your petition that you have made to him." [18] And she said, "Let your servant find favor in your eyes." Then the woman went her way and ate, and her face was no longer sad.

5. Both Hannah and David recalled God's record of steadfast love. Read **Romans 5:1-11**. How can the cross remind us of God's record of steadfast love toward us?

[1]Therefore, since we have been justified by faith, we⁽ᵘ⁾ have peace with God through our Lord Jesus Christ. [2] Through him we have also obtained access by faith⁽ᵘ⁾ into this grace in which

we stand, and we rejoice in hope of the glory of God. ³ Not only that, but we rejoice in our sufferings, knowing that suffering produces endurance, ⁴ and endurance produces character, and character produces hope, ⁵ and hope does not put us to shame, because God's love has been poured into our hearts through the Holy Spirit who has been given to us.

⁶ For while we were still weak, at the right time Christ died for the ungodly. ⁷ For one will scarcely die for a righteous person — though perhaps for a good person one would dare even to die — ⁸ but God shows his love for us in that while we were still sinners, Christ died for us. ⁹ Since, therefore, we have now been justified by his blood, much more shall we be saved by him from the wrath of God. ¹⁰ For if while we were enemies we were reconciled to God by the death of his Son, much more, now that we are reconciled, shall we be saved by his life.¹¹ More than that, we also rejoice in God through our Lord Jesus Christ, through whom we have now received reconciliation.

Commentary and Teaching

Psalm 13 is a personal lament. David poured out his soul to the Lord. He knew God was his refuge (Psalm 62:8), so during his trial, he did not shy away from sharing his raw thoughts and emotions.

Verses 1-2: "How long…" Long trials can tempt us to feel hopeless, especially when our days are filled with sorrow. God does not forget us, but our emotions can trick us and lead us to say, "… will you forget me forever?" "How long will you hide your face from me?" God hiding His face is an expression of His discipline (Spurgeon, 1993, p. 36). Like a good Father, God disciplines His children—but He never forgets them.

"… How long must I wrestle with my thoughts…" David had been crying out to God for a long time and had received no answer. Wrestling with thoughts and meditating on trouble is exhausting and leads us to "having sorrow in [our] heart all the day." The heaviness of this long-term sorrow left David feeling empty and defeated. What makes hard trial even more painful is when our enemies "are exalted over us" and mock us in our pain. David was being mocked, probably by Saul, who was threatening to kill him. His "how longs" express that he could not see an end in sight. So, just as Hannah "wept bitterly and prayed to the Lord" when she was mocked over her pain in 1 Samuel 1:1-18, David did the same in this psalm.

Verses 3-4: David's complaints turned into asks — he still clung to the hope that God might "Consider and answer" him. We know God sees us, and one purpose of our trial is that we may cry out to the One who loves to consider and answer us. David appealed to God's faithful character and boldly asked God to respond. He asked God to "give light to his eyes." This may mean that David was writing this during a time of sickness or physical threat. He may have been asking God to literally open his eyes and save his physical life.

Most commentators believe it has spiritual implications too. We know that light has a rich background in the Old Testament; it often symbolizes truth, hope and the presence of God. Jesus taught, "The eye is the lamp of the body" (Matthew 6:22). The eye gives way to our perspective of faith. David's perspective is dark. He saw no hope. This often leads to emptiness, heaviness, and despair. God, the true light (1 John 1:5), can "give light to [our] eyes." He can give truth, hope, and promise to our perspective. We desperately need God's presence and light in all its live-saving forms, "lest [we] sleep in death" and despair. Again, David thought of the pain of his enemies rejoicing and begged God to act.

Verses 5-6: After pouring out his heart, David turned to the anchor of God's promises; he resolved he could trust in the steadfast love of God. The psalm does not say that David received an answer to his question of "How long," but he was able to express his anguish and grief, while he simultaneously experienced peace as he trusted the eternal love of God that surpasses every trial's length.

So, "How Long?" Not long enough that God's unfailing love would run out. No trial will ever last longer than God's unfailing love will endure. On this side of the cross, we know the fulfillment of David's hope. If we are in Christ, we too can "trust in the God of our salvation." "For God shows His love for us in this, that while we were still sinners, Christ died for us" (Romans 5:8). The cross of Christ, God's display of "unfailing love," gives light and grace to our heart and vision in the darkest times.

Finally, David resolved to sing to the Lord. Sometimes, an outward expression of the heart can release the heaviness of our inward struggle. David had been "wrestling with his thoughts" all day long, but singing truth led to relief and joy in the Lord. He sang because "God had dealt bountifully with him" or "He has been good to me" (NIV). He reflected on God's dealing with him in the past, and as he recalled God's goodness, he was able to have confidence in God's dealing with him in the future. David knew his days had been preordained and "dealt" with according to the steadfast love of God.

How do we speak to God during a seemingly never-ending trial? Pour out your heart to the Lord with your "How Longs?" He is your refuge. He hears your laments and receives them as worship as you entrust your cares to Him. And after you have poured out and pleaded with God, pray He would give light to your eyes so that your heart would trust Him. No matter "how long," "He works all things for the good of those who love Him" (Romans 8:28), and at the cross, "He has dealt bountifully with [us]."

Application and Reflection

1. What in this psalm is personal to you right now?

2. In verse 6, David says "I will sing" to the Lord. How does outwardly singing the truths of God help us keep a truthful perspective?

3. Can you think of a time when, during painful circumstances, God gave you hope and confidence in His steadfast love? What did you learn about God during that time?

4. How can this psalm of lament guide our worship during times of suffering and trial?

Based on your observation and interpretation of Psalm 13, how would YOU pray this prayer? If this psalm applies to you today, take some time to journal through or pray this psalm, based on your own thoughts and circumstances.

Memory Verse for this week:
Psalm 1:1 Blessed is the man who walks not in the counsel of the wicked,
nor stands in the way of sinners, nor sits in the seat of scoffers;

Psalm 51

Observation and Interpretation

Read Psalm 51 and consider the following questions.

[1]Have mercy on me, O God,
  according to your steadfast love;
according to your abundant mercy
  blot out my transgressions.
[2] Wash me thoroughly from my iniquity,
  and cleanse me from my sin!
[3] For I know my transgressions,
  and my sin is ever before me.
[4] Against you, you only, have I sinned
  and done what is evil in your sight,
so that you may be justified in your words
  and blameless in your judgment.
[5] Behold, I was brought forth in iniquity,
  and in sin did my mother conceive me.
[6] Behold, you delight in truth in the inward being,
  and you teach me wisdom in the secret heart.
[7] Purge me with hyssop, and I shall be clean;
  wash me, and I shall be whiter than snow.
[8] Let me hear joy and gladness;
  let the bones that you have broken rejoice.
[9] Hide your face from my sins,
  and blot out all my iniquities.
[10] Create in me a clean heart, O God,
  and renew a right[b] spirit within me.
[11] Cast me not away from your presence,
  and take not your Holy Spirit from me.

¹² Restore to me the joy of your salvation,
  and uphold me with a willing spirit.
¹³ Then I will teach transgressors your ways,
  and sinners will return to you.
¹⁴ Deliver me from bloodguiltiness, O God,
  O God of my salvation,
  and my tongue will sing aloud of your righteousness.
¹⁵ O Lord, open my lips,
  and my mouth will declare your praise.
¹⁶ For you will not delight in sacrifice, or I would give it;
  you will not be pleased with a burnt offering.
¹⁷ The sacrifices of God are a broken spirit;
  a broken and contrite heart, O God, you will not despise.
¹⁸ Do good to Zion in your good pleasure;
  build up the walls of Jerusalem;
¹⁹ then will you delight in right sacrifices,
  in burnt offerings and whole burnt offerings;
  then bulls will be offered on your altar.

1. List the words and phrases David uses to describe his sin and its effects.

2. List words and phrases David uses to describe God's forgiveness and restoration and their effects.

3. The heading for this psalm tells us that David wrote Psalm 51 after an experience of grievous sin and profound forgiveness recorded in 2 Samuel 12. David knew God was a redeemer and a healer who passes over our sins (2 Samuel 12:13). Read **Romans 3:23-26**. What do you learn from these verses about how and why God "passed over" David's sin?

23 for all have sinned and fall short of the glory of God, 24 and are justified by his grace as a gift, through the redemption that is in Christ Jesus, 25 whom God put forward as a propitiation by his blood, to be received by faith. This was to show God's righteousness, because in his divine forbearance he had passed over former sins. 26 It was to show his righteousness at the present time, so that he might be just and the justifier of the one who has faith in Jesus.

3. What did David say his response would be after God restored him? (Psalm 51:13-17)

Why do you think this is his response?

4. Verses 16-17 explain that it is not a sacrifice God desires, but a "broken and contrite heart." Look up these verses in several different translations. What do you think it means to have a broken and contrite heart?

5. In verses 18-19, David prays for God's people (Zion). Summarize his request in your own words.

What do you think the connection is between this prayer and the rest of the psalm?

Commentary and Teaching

In Psalm 51, David laments to God over his sin and asks for forgiveness. It's difficult to have these kinds of conversations with God — but what David shows us in this psalm is that confession, repentance, and grief over sin can lead to humility and worship. When we confess our sin to God, we acknowledge that He alone is holy, and only the work of Christ is worthy to secure our forgiveness.

In many Bibles, the heading of this psalm says something like, "when Nathan the prophet went to him, after he had gone into Bathsheba." The context for that specific event is 2 Samuel 12.

As David reflected on his sin, he used repetition and imagery to express his desperation. "*Blot out* my transgressions, *Wash* me, *Cleanse* me, *purge* me, *take not your holy spirit* from me, *restore* me, *create* in me a clean heart, *cast me not* away…" There is a lot that can be said about these images individually, but collectively, the repetition causes David's deep emotions to leap off the page. This psalm can help give us words when we mourn over our sin and long for the comfort, cleansing, and restoration to joy that only Jesus can provide.

Verses 1-2: David started by asking God for mercy. He didn't ask for mercy depending on his asking, his own ability to do better, or his work or goodness. He asked according to what he knew about God's character; "According to your steadfast love" or "great compassion" (NLT). When we ask for forgiveness, we fully depend on God's great mercy toward us in Christ.

"Blot out my transgressions…" The term "blot" refers to "blotting out of a book" as one would need his record of debt blotted out (The Songs, 2015, 109). The ESV Study Bible explains that throughout the psalm, words like "wash, cleanse, and blot out" refer to the ceremonial cleansing needed to come into God's presence. Jesus offers us this full and complete cleansing. Colossians 2:14 tells us that Jesus' work "… [cancelled] the record of debt that stood against us with its legal demands. This he set aside, nailing to the cross." When we see David's plea for renewal and purity, we can thank God for His indescribable gift through Jesus.

Verses 3-6: Verse 3 says, "My sin is ever before me," or as the NLT says, "it haunts me day and night." Matthew Henry said: "He had such a deep sense of it [his sin] that he was continually thinking of it with sorrow and shame. His contrition for his sin was not a slight sudden passion, but an abiding grief (1706, Psalm 51)." This verse describes the feeling of a cloud of condemnation and painful reminders of his sin. Everywhere he looked, he was reminded of his guilt, and he longed for the relief and cleansed conscience that only God could grant.

David acknowledged, "against you only have I sinned." David's sin hurt many people, but our sin is always primarily against God. Our sin separates us from God and breaks His rule and law. Tim Keller explains: "… Sin is like treason. If you try to overthrow your country, you may harm or kill individuals in the process, but you will be tried for treason because you have betrayed the entire country that nurtured you. So, every sin is cosmic treason- it is overthrowing the rule of the one to whom you owe everything" (The Songs, 2015, 108). It is important to seek forgiveness from others whom our sin has affected, but only after we have sought reconciliation with God.

Then David worshiped God's righteous character as he said, "...so that you may be justified in your words and blameless in your judgment." We can learn from David's process of repentance as it shows us to not focus only on our sin, but on God's perfect judgment, righteousness, and holiness. Becoming aware of our sin can lead us to worship when we compare ourselves to His holy, perfect character.

David further reflected on his condition, "Behold, I was brought forth in iniquity," or as the NLT says, "I was born a sinner." "And in sin did my mother conceive me." Paul echoed this reality in his letter to the Romans: "For all have sinned and fall short of the glory of God" (Romans 3:23). Even so, "Behold," David marveled, "you delight in truth in the inward being, and teach me wisdom in the secret heart." Our condition is dark, but God still desires and requires deep inward purity; only He can change us from the inside.

Verses 7-12: No matter how or how much we have sinned; God forgives us and restores us when we ask. David pleaded for this in verses 7-12. God gave David an earnest desire for the purity that we know is only achieved in Christ. He asked, "purge me with hyssop and I shall be clean." He is referring to a hyssop plant and its use in the cleansing ceremony mentioned in Leviticus 14:6 and Numbers 19:6. David pleaded, "wash me, and I shall be whiter than snow." Snow starts out as white, but can melt, get dirty, and become discolored (Spurgeon, 1993, p. 212). So, David asked for an eternal purity whiter than snow.

It is hard to describe the longing felt during repentance, but David articulated it well. He asked desperately and repeatedly to be cleansed and washed from the weight and hard-heartedness caused by sin. From the New Testament, we know this is possible because of Jesus. Titus 3:4 tells us, "when the goodness and lovingkindness of God our Savior appeared, He saved us, not because of the works done by us in righteousness, but according to His own mercy, by the washing of regeneration and renewal of the Holy Spirit, whom He poured out on us richly through Jesus Christ our Savior, so that being justified by His grace we might become heirs according to the hope of eternal life." When we ask for cleansing from our sin, we can do it with confidence in the work of Christ.

David understood that what he needed was not to merely 'do better,' but he needed a new heart. Only the Creator God can create a new heart (Spurgeon, 1993, p. 213). David longed for this "right spirit," to experience the joy of his salvation and the presence of God. He knew that even in his abiding grief, God could grant him sustaining and eternal joy. If we belong to Christ, we know the joy and blessed humility that comes with being loved, redeemed, and accepted by Him. When our sin overwhelms us, we don't always feel this joy, but God can restore this to us.

Verses 13-17: David told God that if his request for forgiveness and restoration was granted, he would be an agent of this restoration for others. He explains, "Then I will teach transgressors your ways, and sinners will return to you." The NLT says in verse 14, "Forgive me for shedding blood, then I will sing of your forgiveness." When we experience God's forgiveness, He gives us a desire to help others experience His grace and forgiveness as we have.

In 16-17, David acknowledged that God's desire was not primarily for a rote sacrifice or act of obedience. God wanted David's heart. He expressed with deep and hopeful confidence that God "will not despise" a "broken and contrite heart." This is a heart full of godly sorrow over sin. Not a worldly grief merely concerned with consequences, but a godly sorrow that is genuinely brokenhearted over offending a holy God (2 Corinthians 7:10). God can produce this in us, and when He does, He will not "despise" it or turn away — He will accept it gently and tenderly by His grace. This is a precious comfort for us.

Verses 18-19: Lastly, David asked God that his sin would not affect God's people (Zion). He asked for worship to be restored in the temple. David was an influential person, and he knew his actions could have a ripple effect. When we learn about our sin, we should pray for the church. We are "members of one another" (Romans 12:4) and our actions affect one another. David's words show us that our desire and prayer for restoration should include those our sins may have affected.

Application and Reflection

David's example of repentance includes:
1. No defensiveness but an appeal only to God's mercy (vs. 1-2).
2. An acknowledgment that his sin is against God (vs 4).
3. Grieving over his sin rather than grieving the consequences of his sin.
4. Not a goal to "do better," but a plea for God to restore him and "create in him a new heart... uphold him with a willing spirit" and restore his joy (vs 10-12).
5. A focus on God in repentance that causes him to praise and worship the righteousness of God (vs 14-15).
6. After restoration, a desire to teach others about the mercy and righteousness of God (vs. 13-16).

1. How does David's example of repentance inspire you to grow in your own repentance?

2. What benefits of God's forgiveness and restoration stand out to you? Why?

3. How do you read this psalm in light of taking refuge in our Justifier and Savior Jesus Christ who is on the throne? (Psalm 2)

Based on your observation and interpretation, how would YOU pray this prayer? Take some time to journal through or pray this psalm, based on your own thoughts and circumstances.

Thanksgiving

Psalm 30

Observation and Interpretation

Read Psalm 30 and consider the following questions.

¹I will extol you, O Lord, for you have drawn me up
  and have not let my foes rejoice over me.
²O Lord my God, I cried to you for help,
  and you have healed me.
³O Lord, you have brought up my soul from Sheol;
  you restored me to life from among those who go down to
the pit.
⁴Sing praises to the Lord, O you his saints,
  and give thanks to his holy name.
⁵For his anger is but for a moment,
  and his favor is for a lifetime.
Weeping may tarry for the night,
  but joy comes with the morning.
⁶As for me, I said in my prosperity,
  "I shall never be moved."
⁷By your favor, O Lord,
  you made my mountain stand strong;
you hid your face;
  I was dismayed.
⁸To you, O Lord, I cry,
  and to the Lord I plead for mercy:
⁹"What profit is there in my death,

if I go down to the pit?
Will the dust praise you?
  Will it tell of your faithfulness?
10 Hear, O Lord, and be merciful to me!
  O Lord, be my helper!"
11 You have turned for me my mourning into dancing;
  you have loosed my sackcloth
  and clothed me with gladness,
12 that my glory may sing your praise and not be silent.
  O Lord my God, I will give thanks to you forever!

1. List the phrases David uses to thank God for His rescue in verses 1-3.

2. What aspects of God's character does David praise in verses 4-5?

3. In verses 6-7, David recalls a time when he became proud and forgot the grace of God. Describe his experience in your own words. (Consulting different Bible translations may be helpful. Resources like Biblegateway.com can help with this).

4. What is David's conclusion about who sustains and gives joy in vs. 11-12?

What is his resolution and application in verse 12?

Commentary and Teaching

Psalms of thanksgiving give us prayer prompts that lead us to a heart of gratitude. In Psalm 30, David reflected in awe over the many ways God's presence had blessed and rescued him. He models prayerful and reflective thanksgiving over God's gracious salvation in the trials and joys of life.

Verses 1-3: David thanked and praised God for rescuing him. He seems to talk about a physical rescue. David was often in life-threatening situations. God can protect us from physical harm, and this is what He had done for David. He explained that it was an answer to prayer that God had done this: "I cried to you for help, and you have healed me." God does all things for His glory and our good, and sometimes, this means protecting us from physical harm.

He continued and said, "you have brought up my soul from Sheol; you restored me to life from those who go down to the pit." God had saved David from death. David was not specific about the nature of the deliverance he experienced; this is by design. The psalm draws us to sing along with David as we worship God, not only for His deliverance of David, but His deliverance of us. God can rescue us from physical harm, death, and spiritual death. For those in Christ, Jesus has taken care of our greatest need on the cross. He has brought us from death and "restored [us] to life." Paul expanded and said, "But God, being rich in mercy, because of the great love with which he loved us, even when we were dead in our trespasses, made us alive together with Christ- by grace you have been saved" Ephesians 2:5.

Verses 4-5: As David reflected on God's salvation, he wrote about the ways it came through God's intimate care in the ups and downs of his life. God lovingly ordains the seasons where we weep through the night, the ones where joy permeates, and all the circumstances in between. He said, "For His anger is but for a moment, but His favor is for a lifetime. Weeping may tarry for the night, but joy comes in the morning." This is a beautiful description of God's goodness toward us. Many of us can look back on our lives and see highs and lows. We can recall times of weeping when we couldn't understand what God was doing, and times when our joy was restored. But overall, it's God's favor that marks His plan for His children. The Message paraphrases verse 5a, "He gets angry once in a while, but across a lifetime there is only love" (MSG). When we reflect on our years of knowing Jesus, we can often see God's hand of discipline. But in our looking back, we should ask God to help us reflect with thanksgiving to see the overarching theme of His favor and love. How is this true of your life? Are you in a season of weeping? There is a firm foundation for us in God's kind providence. The weeping and joy all come through the nail-scarred hands of favor and love.

Verses 6-10: In the middle of this psalm of Thanksgiving, David confessed that he didn't always have a heart of thanks. He recalled a time he responded to God's deliverance with pride. He became overconfident and thought his success was because of something he had done. Whether it is consciously or unconsciously, we can all subtly slip into thinking, "I've got this." We can believe in an illusion of our own control and security apart from the grace of God. Thankfully, God doesn't let us live so deceived. God disciplined David, but David knew God's salvation offers mercy and rescue for this kind of failure, too. So, David responded to his realization of his sin by appealing to God's mercy again.

He cried out to God, saying, "You hid your face; I was dismayed. To you O lord, I cry… and to the Lord I plead for mercy." David realized where true unshakable confidence is found. Tim Keller explains, "…God shakes our confidence in our earthly life so that we can yearn for ourselves a heavenly life, where our joy is truly unshakable and where our wailing will be turned to dancing" (The Songs, 2015, p. 55).

Verses 11-12: David praised God in verse 11 that "he has turned my mourning into dancing." God restores our "dancing" and joy in our lives, and one day He will take away our mourning forever. He will take away our clothes of mourning or "loose our sackcloth" and "clothe [us] with gladness." Revelation 22:4 promises, "…He will wipe away every tear from their eyes, and there will no longer be any death; there will no longer be any mourning, nor crying, or pain; the first things have passed away." When God restores our "dancing" in our earthly lives, it is a shadow of the eternal joy He will grant to us in heaven.

God's salvation prompts our deep gratitude; His grace is more than enough to care for us in every season we encounter. Through success or failure, mourning or joy, in Jesus Christ we are held by favor and love. We can give thanks for this, "and not be silent." God's deliverance to us, both in earthly trials and in our salvation, is meant to prompt our private, public, and joyful thanks to Him.

Application and Reflection

1. Though we all experience periods of "mourning and dancing," God's overall plan for our lives is marked by His favor. How have you seen evidence of this in your life?

2. Think of a time when, like David, you witnessed God's power of salvation. What did this event teach you about God?

3. Is there an area of your life in which your attitude is like David's when he said, "I shall never be moved"? How does David's prayer challenge your perspective in this area?

5. As you reflect on this Psalm, and your own personal experience, how is thanksgiving an antidote to a prideful heart?

4. What is a practical way you can share God's goodness with others and "not be silent" because of His grace to you? (Psalm 32:12).

Based on your observation and interpretation, how would YOU pray this prayer? Take some time to journal through or pray this psalm, based on your own thoughts and circumstances.

Memory Verse for this week:
Psalm 1:2: but his delight is in the law of the LORD, and on his law he meditates day and night.

Psalm 32

Observation and Interpretation

Read Psalm 32 and consider the following questions.

[1]Blessed is the one whose transgression is forgiven,
  whose sin is covered.
[2] Blessed is the man against whom the Lord counts no
iniquity,
  and in whose spirit there is no deceit.
[3] For when I kept silent, my bones wasted away
  through my groaning all day long.
[4] For day and night your hand was heavy upon me;
  my strength was dried up as by the heat of summer. *Selah*
[5] I acknowledged my sin to you,
  and I did not cover my iniquity;
I said, "I will confess my transgressions to the Lord,"
  and you forgave the iniquity of my sin. *Selah*
[6] Therefore let everyone who is godly
  offer prayer to you at a time when you may be found;
surely in the rush of great waters,
  they shall not reach him.
[7] You are a hiding place for me;
  you preserve me from trouble;
  you surround me with shouts of deliverance. *Selah*
[8] I will instruct you and teach you in the way you should go;
  I will counsel you with my eye upon you.
[9] Be not like a horse or a mule, without understanding,
  which must be curbed with bit and bridle,
  or it will not stay near you.

[10] Many are the sorrows of the wicked,
  but steadfast love surrounds the one who trusts in the Lord.
[11] Be glad in the Lord, and rejoice, O righteous,
  and shout for joy, all you upright in heart!

1. Look up verses 1 and 2 in different translations. Describe the benefits and blessings that come with forgiveness.

2. In verses 3 and 4, David recalls an experience when he was reluctant to confess his sin. In your own words, describe David's experience of conviction and repentance in verses 3-5.

3. Read verses 6 and 7 again. Now read **2 Corinthians 5:21** and **Colossians 3:3-4** and consider: how is the cross of Christ a "hiding place" for us?

2 Corinthians 5:21

[21] For our sake he made him to be sin who knew no sin, so that in him we might become the righteousness of God.

Colossians 3:3-4

[3] For you have died, and your life is hidden with Christ in God. [4] When Christ who is your life appears, then you also will appear with him in glory.

4. Describe the results of:
God hiding David's sin —

David attempting to hide his own sin —

5. The voice changes in verses 8-9 to God speaking. Describe what He says in your own words.

How does this connect with the repentance in the previous verses?

Commentary and Teaching

Psalm 32 is a thanksgiving psalm. David expressed his thanks to God for forgiveness of sin. He described the blessings of forgiveness as he recalled an experience of his repentance. This psalm offers a script for us when we are grateful for God's forgiveness in Christ; it helps us seek the humility and worship that comes with thankfulness for our salvation.

Verses 1-2: Deep blessing and joy are granted to us when our sins are forgiven. The NLT says: "Oh what joy for those whose disobedience has been forgiven." God "puts our sin out of sight." Psalm 103:12 says, "As far as the east is from the west, so the Lord has removed our transgressions from us." We have peace with God when we stand in His grace.

When we experience the freedom of forgiveness, we can live as those "in whose spirit is no deceit," or, as the NLT says, "whose lives are lived in complete honesty." Forgiveness allows for authenticity when we acknowledge we are, as Tim Keller says, "… more sinful and flawed in ourselves than we ever dared believe, yet at the very same time we are more loved and accepted in Jesus Christ than we ever dared hope." The cross allows us to be honest before God and others about who we truly are and where hope is found.

Our thoughts can often stray to self-justification as we try to think of ourselves as "pretty good." We can try to create an inward "peace" for ourselves by telling ourselves we are better than we really are. Living with this false perception of ourselves is tiresome, and it doesn't offer real peace. But as we stand in the grace of God, we are free to be both honest and hopeful about who we are in Christ.

Verses 3-4: David recalled a time when he was reluctant to confess his sin. He describes physical and emotional anguish: "for when I kept silent my bones wasted away through my groaning all day long." David discerned this pain was "[God's] hand of discipline… heavy on [him]" (NLT). We can't hide our sins on our own, it only causes harm to ourselves, others, and our relationship with God. Only God can hide our sin for us.

Verse 5-7: David shares that he finally acknowledged his sin and "did not cover [his] iniquity." God forgave him. His response was to tell others about the forgiveness of God so they might turn to Him while they still have the chance. He said, "let everyone who is godly offer a prayer to you at a time while you may be found." This is a pattern we have seen in David's life: when he experiences the character and grace of God, he longs for others to see it, too.

In previous verses, David had been using words that describe an attempt at "hiding" or "covering" his sin on his own. When he reflects on the power of God hiding his sin, he concludes with praise: "You (God) are a hiding place for me, you preserve me from trouble; you surround me with shouts of deliverance." Charles Spurgeon noted: "Observe that the same man who in the fourth verse was oppressed by the presence of God here finds a shelter in Him. See what honest confession and full forgiveness will do! The Gospel of substitution makes Him our refuge who would have otherwise been our judge" (1993, Vol 1, p. 125). The object of David's faith was God's abundant mercy and ability to cover sins completely. What he didn't yet realize is that this would be fulfilled in Jesus Christ. When we confess our sin, God hides it in the cross of Christ. Christ's righteousness hides and covers our unrighteousness (2 Corinthians 5:21), and we are protected from the harm and deep sorrow that comes with sin's consequence. God's complete salvation and covering through Christ warrants shouts and songs of His merciful deliverance.

Verses 8-9: The voice changes here. Most commentators believe this is God speaking to David. He gave a warning, "Be not like a horse or mule, without understanding, which must be curbed with bit and bridle or it will not stay near you." This transition seems to explain that God not only desires repentance and forgiveness, but He wants us in a full relationship with Him. Sometimes God gives us an experience of discipline (like the one David wrote about in the psalm) so that we might be humbled to trust, love, and follow Him. God does not want us to resist His counsel and wisdom like a horse or mule that is forced against its own will. He wants us to obey out of a love for Him.

Verses 10-11: David summarized his experience, "many are the sorrows of the wicked." We read about his experience of sorrow in verses 3 and 4. Many are the sorrows of those who try to hide their sin. We cannot hide our sin ourselves, and attempting to do so causes great pain. But praise Jesus, our Hiding Place! "Steadfast love surrounds the one who trusts in the Lord." When we confess our sin to God, He hides our sin in Christ. He accomplished reconciliation with us through Jesus. Our response should be to confess and repent quickly, thank Him and praise Him, and be filled with His joy. Then, as David was, we will be compelled to tell others to do the same. In the last line, David cried out in deep gratitude, "Be glad in the Lord, and rejoice, O righteous, and shout for joy, all you upright in heart!"

Application and Reflection

1. David tried to hide his sin and felt his "bones wasting away." When he confessed and allowed God to hide his sin, he found joy. Have you ever experienced this? If so, describe the occasion below.

2. Which of the blessings of forgiveness stand out to you? Why?

3. Think of a blessing of forgiveness you would like to experience more of in your life. How will the desire for this blessing inform your prayer life?

4. How might singing or praying this psalm guide the way we thank God for His forgiveness in Christ?

Based on your observation and interpretation, how would YOU pray this prayer? Take some time to journal through or pray this psalm, based on your own thoughts and circumstances.

Wisdom

Psalm 131

Observation and Interpretation

Read Psalm 131 and consider the following questions.

¹O Lord, my heart is not lifted up;
  my eyes are not raised too high;
I do not occupy myself with things
  too great and too marvelous for me.
²But I have calmed and quieted my soul,
  like a weaned child with its mother;
  like a weaned child is my soul within me.
³O Israel, hope in the Lord
  from this time forth and forevermore.

1. Consider consulting different translations of verse 1. Then, describe David's perspective from verse 1 in your own words:

2. Here is some context for verse 2 from Charles Spurgeon:

"Eastern people put off the time of weaning far later than we do, and we may conclude that the process grows none the easier by being postponed. At last there must be an end to the suckling period, and then the battle begins: the child is denied his comfort, and therefore frets and worries, flies into tantrums or sinks into sulks. It is facing its first great sorrow, and is in sore distress. Yet time brings not only alleviations, but the ending of the conflict; the boy ere long is quite content to find his nourishment at the table with his brothers, and he feels no lingering wish to return to those dear fountains from which he once sustained his life. He is no longer angry with his mother, but buries his head in that very bosom for which he pined so grievously: he is weaned *of* his mother rather than *from* her." (1993, Vol. 2, p. 286).

Given this context, describe what you think it means for our soul to be "like a weaned child with its mother" versus a nursing child.

3. What was David's final exhortation about where to find hope?

How do you think he came to this conclusion? (Or, how do you think his conclusion is connected to the difficult process in verses 1-2?)

4. Read **Philippians 2:1-11**. How does David's example of contentment and humility point us to Jesus' greater contentment and humility?

[1]So if there is any encouragement in Christ, any comfort from love, any participation in the Spirit, any affection and sympathy, [2]complete my joy by being of the same mind, having the same love, being in full accord and of one mind. [3]Do nothing from selfish ambition or conceit, but in humility count others more significant than yourselves.[4]Let each of you look not only to his own interests, but also to the interests of others. [5]Have this mind among yourselves, which is yours in Christ Jesus, [6]who, though he was in the form of God, did not count equality with God a thing to be grasped, [7]but emptied himself, by taking the form of a servant, being born in the likeness of men. [8]And being found in human form, he humbled himself by becoming obedient to the point of death, even death on a cross.[9]Therefore God has highly exalted him and bestowed on him the name that is above every name, [10]so that at the name of Jesus every knee should bow, in heaven and on earth and under the earth, [11]and every tongue confess that Jesus Christ is Lord, to the glory of God the Father.

Commentary and Teaching

David denounced his pride and pursued contentment and rest in God Himself. He articulated what a humble and content heart looks like. This psalm can give us words and prayers for when we are wrestling with our pride or unmet desires. At the end of this prayer, David painted a picture of wisdom, deep trust, and contentment in the Lord.

Verse 1: David models the process of pursuing humility. Tim Keller said, "The essence of gospel humility is not thinking more of myself or thinking less of myself, it is thinking of myself less." (Keller, 2011, pg. 44). David has learned to think more of God than himself; he shared what *didn't* occupy his mind as he denounced pride and self-centeredness in three ways. He described 1. What his heart was *not* focused on, 2. What his eyes were *not* focused on, 3. What *didn't* occupy him.

He said, "my heart is not lifted up," the NASB says "proud." Pride begins in our hearts. David was saying his heart was not proud; he had a correct view of himself. Then he said, "my eyes are not raised too high." The posture of our hearts leads to the perspective of our "eyes". Spurgeon explains: "What the heart desires, the eyes look for. Where the heart desires, the eyes usually follow. This holy man felt that he did not seek after elevated places where he might gratify his self-esteem, neither did he look down upon others as being inferiors." (1993, Vol. 2, p. 285) Finally, he shared what did not "occupy" him or what he did not act upon. "I have not occupied myself with things too great and marvelous for me." The Message paraphrases this, "I haven't meddled where I have no business or fantasized grandiose plans."

David said his heart was not focused on himself or his ambitions. When we view ourselves as "great," we tend to dwell on, seek, and then act upon great things for ourselves. Many times, the "great and marvelous things" we desire are not bad, but if our hope is in them, we can become distracted from the faithfulness and purpose God calls us to. "Do you seek great things for yourself? Seek them not..." (Jeremiah 45:5). When we are focused on acting on our own plans, we miss the peace-filled fellowship with our Father that we were created for. David elaborated on where his hope *was* placed in the next verse.

Verse 2: David "calmed and quieted his soul." He pursued satisfaction in the Lord and was brought to a place of rest and humility. He wrote of the beauty of a contented, humble heart. In doing so, he compared his heart to a weaned child, satisfied with his mother's presence and companionship.

When a baby is nursing, he is restless and discontent in his mother's arms because he wants, not just his mother, but what his mother can give. A weaned child is denied the comfort of milk, but he is content. He is not anxious about a meal, but he can simply rest with his mother and enjoy her.

David calmed and quieted his soul because his satisfaction was God himself. He was not pursuing great things or accomplishments for his own glory; he was not obsessed with what the future might hold or what God might give him. David was able to rest, content in the presence of his Father.

The image of a weaned child conjures up feelings of rest and quiet contentment. But this peaceful metaphor has a hidden backstory; it's not easy to wean a child. And a similar backstory exists for the content and humble heart that David described.

David's original audience would have been familiar with the amount of challenging work it took to wean a child. In the same way, learning to "be content in every circumstance" (Philippians 4:11) is a long, arduous process for the believer. David's humility and wisdom were learned through trial, waiting, and long-suffering. For much of David's life, he lived with a desire to be the leader of Israel. This was a good desire and one God had called him to. However, much of his time waiting was spent hiding in caves, running from Saul. David had a great calling, but he had to wait and trust God's wisdom. This might have been one of the many trials in David's life that taught him the humility and contentment we see in this psalm.

Of course, we see this example of humility most profoundly in the life of Jesus. Paul's letter to the Philippians instructs us to "Have this mind among yourselves which is yours in Christ Jesus, who though He was in the very form of God, did not count equality with God a thing to be grasped. But he emptied Himself, taking on the form of a servant, being born in the likeness of men. And being found in human form, he humbled himself. Becoming obedient to the point of death, even death on a cross" (Philippians 2:5-8). Jesus was fully God, but in His time on earth, He laid down His right to "occupy himself with great and marvelous things." He came as a baby born in a stable. He was obedient to His earthly parents, and He worked as a carpenter before His ministry began. Everything He did was to please His Heavenly Father (John 8:29). He was obedient to the point of death, for our salvation, so that we might have hope in Him. As our Heavenly Father gently pursues our hearts to help us be content in His presence, we will undoubtedly struggle and stumble. But our hope is in Jesus, who pursued contentment and humility perfectly and without sin on our behalf.

Verse 3: Therefore, David encouraged: "O Israel, Hope in the Lord, From this time forth and forevermore." He experienced the contentment and peace only God could offer, and he yearned for Israel to experience it as he did. Psalm 131 offers us this timeless wisdom: after a long journey of questioning, suffering, confusion, and endurance, a wise and humble heart finds its rest and hope in God Himself. In the presence of our Father, we have genuine joy, peace, and pleasure. We can lay down our desires and dreams for Him. We can place them in His hands, trust Him, and rest.

Application and Reflection

1. What part of David's pursuit of humility and contentment is challenging to you?

2. Has there ever been a time when you put your hope in a set of circumstances instead of the Lord? How did this affect your relationship with God?

3. What steps can you take to "have this mind among you that is yours in Christ Jesus" (Philippians 2:5) and hope and trust God the way the psalmist describes?

Based on your observation and interpretation, how would YOU pray this prayer? Take some time to journal through or pray this psalm, based on your own thoughts and circumstances.

Memory Verse for this week: Psalm 1:3-4 "He is like a tree planted by streams of water that yields its fruit in its season, and its leaf does not wither. In all that he does, he prospers. The wicked are not so, but are like chaff that the wind drives away."

Psalm 73

Observation and Interpretation

Read Psalm 73 and consider the following questions.

¹Truly God is good to Israel,
  to those who are pure in heart.
² But as for me, my feet had almost stumbled,
  my steps had nearly slipped.
³ For I was envious of the arrogant
  when I saw the prosperity of the wicked.
⁴ For they have no pangs until death;
  their bodies are fat and sleek.
⁵ They are not in trouble as others are;
  they are not stricken like the rest of mankind.
⁶ Therefore pride is their necklace;
  violence covers them as a garment.
⁷ Their eyes swell out through fatness;
  their hearts overflow with follies.
⁸ They scoff and speak with malice;
  loftily they threaten oppression.
⁹ They set their mouths against the heavens,
  and their tongue struts through the earth.
¹⁰ Therefore his people turn back to them,
  and find no fault in them.
¹¹ And they say, "How can God know?
  Is there knowledge in the Most High?"
¹² Behold, these are the wicked;

always at ease, they increase in riches.
13 All in vain have I kept my heart clean
  and washed my hands in innocence.
14 For all the day long I have been stricken
  and rebuked every morning.
15 If I had said, "I will speak thus,"
  I would have betrayed the generation of your children.
16 But when I thought how to understand this,
  it seemed to me a wearisome task,
17 until I went into the sanctuary of God;
  then I discerned their end.
18 Truly you set them in slippery places;
  you make them fall to ruin.
19 How they are destroyed in a moment,
  swept away utterly by terrors!
20 Like a dream when one awakes,
  O Lord, when you rouse yourself, you despise them as
phantoms.
21 When my soul was embittered,
  when I was pricked in heart,
22 I was brutish and ignorant;
  I was like a beast toward you.
23 Nevertheless, I am continually with you;
  you hold my right hand.
24 You guide me with your counsel,
  and afterward you will receive me to glory.
25 Whom have I in heaven but you?
  And there is nothing on earth that I desire besides you.
26 My flesh and my heart may fail,
  but God is the strength[b] of my heart and my portion forever.
27 For behold, those who are far from you shall perish;
  you put an end to everyone who is unfaithful to you.
28 But for me it is good to be near God;
  I have made the Lord God my refuge,
  that I may tell of all your works.

1. Asaph declares: "Truly God is good to Israel." Then he reflects on a time when he had forgotten God's goodness. What was the result described in verses 4-15?

2. Describe what causes a turning point in his thoughts? (Starting in verse 16).

3. Asaph speaks about the reality that sometimes the **wicked prosper, but the righteous suffer.** Read **Matthew 20:17-28.** From this passage in Matthew and/or others, give an example of the reality Asaph describes from the life of Jesus.

[17] And as Jesus was going up to Jerusalem, he took the twelve disciples aside, and on the way he said to them, [18] "See, we are going up to Jerusalem. And the Son of Man will be delivered over to the chief priests and scribes, and they will condemn him to death [19] and deliver him over to the Gentiles to be mocked and flogged and crucified, and he will be raised on the third day."

[20] Then the mother of the sons of Zebedee came up to him with her sons, and kneeling before him she asked him for something. [21] And he said to her, "What do you want?" She said to him, "Say that these two sons of mine are to sit, one at your right hand and one at your left, in your kingdom." [22] Jesus answered, "You do not know what you are asking. Are you able to drink the cup that I am to drink?" They said to him, "We are able." [23] He said to them, "You will drink my cup, but to sit at my right hand and at my left is not mine to grant, but it is for those for whom it has been prepared by my Father." [24] And when the ten heard

it, they were indignant at the two brothers. ²⁵ But Jesus called them to him and said, "You know that the rulers of the Gentiles lord it over them, and their great ones exercise authority over them.²⁶ It shall not be so among you. But whoever would be great among you must be your servant, ²⁷ and whoever would be first among you must be your slave, ²⁸ even as the Son of Man came not to be served but to serve, and to give his life as a ransom for many."

4. What does Asaph conclude about where he should find peace and satisfaction?

Commentary and Teaching

Psalm 73 is a wisdom psalm written by Asaph. Asaph was a worship leader in the time of David whose job was to write songs for God's people. There are themes in Psalm 73 that we may recognize from Ecclesiastes, Proverbs, or other wisdom books. In Ecclesiastes 1 Solomon says.. "everything is vanity," and Proverbs 11:18 says, "The wicked earns deceptive wages, but one who sows righteousness gets a sure reward." In this psalm, Asaph gave a glimpse of his journey from wrestling to peace. He prayerfully questioned and struggled with the apparent ease of those who don't seek God, and his plea led him to God's timeless wisdom: God's presence is the only true, lasting treasure.

Verse 1: Asaph knew the truth. God is good to His people, Israel. He declared this plainly even though he was struggling with temptation. God is good to the pure in heart- those who seek Him.

Verses 2-3: Asaph then reflected on a time when he doubted God's goodness to Israel. He says, "I almost stumbled." What caused this? He was envious of the lives of the wicked; he referred to those who do not follow God and His ways. Specifically, he seemed to be envious of their apparent prosperity and ease of life.

Verses 4-9: These verses list characteristics of how the wicked, from the outside, appear to be thriving. These descriptions turn out to be timeless. The "wicked" appear to have painless lives and their bodies are beautiful and healthy (vs. 4). They don't have to worry about everyday things, they have powerful connections to get them out of trouble (vs. 5). They handle things with pride and violence (vs. 6). They seem to have everything they could ever wish for (vs. 7). They threaten and oppress others with their words. They mock God and those who love Him.

Asaph was jealous of the wicked; we are often guilty of this too. We want their wealth, popularity, and ease of life. Sometimes circumstances like this shine a light in our hearts to show us what we are treasuring.

Jesus taught, "Do not lay up for yourselves treasures on earth, where moth and rust destroy and where thieves break in and steal. But lay up for yourselves treasures in heaven, where neither moth nor rust destroy and thieves do not break in and steal. **For where your treasure is, there your heart will be also** (Matthew 6:19-21).

At this point in the psalm, it seems Asaph's heart has followed the earthly treasure. This is revealed further in the next verses.

Verses 13-15: "All in vain have I kept my heart clean…" Asaph questioned, 'why do I even serve God?' The "wicked" don't serve God and yet they seem to have a better life than him. He wanted to know, "what's in it for me?" Keller explains: "But this unmasks his heart. His obedience was not a way of pleasing God but rather a means of getting God to please him" (The Songs, 2015, 168). We often can serve God with the motivation of receiving something from Him. But believers in Christ are called to suffer for the sake of Christ (Romans 5:3). So, there will be times when it seems that those who do not follow Christ have everything they want, while we as Christ followers are suffering.

We see this play out in the life of Jesus and His disciples. When Jesus is betrayed, it appears that the wicked have the upper hand while Jesus is called to suffer. Judas was making connections with the religious elite in order to gain wealth, and the religious elite oppressed Jesus, who, in their minds, was a threat to their power. The "wicked" seemed on top. Those who persecuted and eventually killed Jesus for greed, jealousy, and power seemed to get everything they wanted. The disciples were left scattered and confused as they watched their Messiah suffer.

How do we understand this? Asaph modeled how to process this in the next verses.

Verses 16-20: Asaph entered the sanctuary of God, and His presence granted truth and light to Asaph's bitter heart. When we try to understand the condition of this world, what we see on the news, or our personal suffering, it is truly a "wearisome task." We must draw near to God and His truth in our wrestling.

Asaph had been focusing on the present life of those who don't know God. When he entered the sanctuary of God, he discerned "their end."

"Truly you set them in slippery places..." The success and wealth of the wicked is temporary. In the "end," they will fall. We read this in Psalm 1: "Therefore the wicked will not stand in the judgment." This is heavy to think about- those who do not know God and seek their treasure in this life only will "fall to ruin." Though they spend their life on earth at ease, their earthly treasure will be destroyed and they will spend eternity separated from God.

When we wake up from a dream, we often laugh at its silliness. The NLT translates verse 20: "When you arise, O Lord, you will laugh at their silly ideas, as a person laughs at dreams in the morning." The celebrity status and wealth of those who don't know Jesus are like a dream. They are fleeting and temporary.

Verses 23-28: In these verses, Asaph first acknowledged God's grace and kindness to him in his doubt. He shared how he was bitter, and like a "beast" before God. But God still didn't leave him in his doubting and wrestling. This reality can give us hope when we experience doubt and temptation. God can handle our questions, "he is continually with [us], he holds [our] right hand." Asaph "nearly slipped," but God held him. Asaph realizes that treasure is found in God himself. "Whom have I in heaven but you?" For the believer, our joy is in Christ. God, in His grace, gives us good gifts on earth. But these gifts are only a shadow of the true substance- our treasure in heaven.

This proved to be true in the life of Christ and His disciples as well. **Three days after the crucifixion of Jesus, "The end" of the wicked and the hope of those who trust in Jesus was revealed. The resurrection truly changes everything.**

Paul taught that for the Christian, if Christ has not been raised, and we hope in Christ for this life only, then "we are of all men most to be pitied. **But now, Christ has been raised from the dead**" (1 Corinthians 15:19- 20). And He has secured for us an inheritance that is "imperishable, undefiled, and unfading, kept in heaven for [us]" (1 Peter 1:4). This is what the resurrection means for those who are in Christ. It's what Asaph meant when he said, "Whom have I in heaven but you? There is nothing on earth that I desire besides you." Our treasure is Christ, and if we trust in Him, He is secured for us because of His life, death, and resurrection. Our hope, and Asaph's hope, is in Jesus.

We may continue to struggle to remember where our treasure is. The treasure of the world will continue to be appealing, especially when we are suffering. Asaph knew this too, but he looked forward with hope. "My flesh and my heart may fail..." We can acknowledge, with Asaph, that we need help to hope in Christ. We can also be mindful that our flesh and the desires we have on this earth are fleeting and will certainly fail us. But, "God is the strength of my heart and my portion forever." When we struggle with temptation, God will hold us up. We can confess our jealousy and wrestle with the truth before Him. He is the strength of our hearts.

He is also the strength of our portion. The Holman Bible Dictionary defines portion as "our allowance, allotment, ration, or share..." Our portion in heaven and on earth is Jesus and knowing Him. God guards our portion in heaven through our faith in Christ's death and resurrection... "ready to be revealed in the last time..." (1 Peter 1:5).

Regarding our secure inheritance, Paul concluded that "the sufferings of this present time are not worth comparing with the glory that is to be revealed to us" (Romans 8:18). Asaph concluded the same; as the psalm ends, he declares, "For me, it is good to be near God."

Application and Reflection

1. Have you ever wrestled with the truth about God?

 What can we learn from the process of Asaph's wrestling and receiving God's wisdom?

2. Asaph was finally at peace when he realized "the end" of the wicked and the hope of the righteous. He was able to proclaim, "God is the strength of my heart and my portion forever." Read **1 Peter 1:3-5, 18-21**, and **Philippians 3:7-14** and consider: how do the life, death, and resurrection of Christ secure the hope that Asaph mentions?

1 Peter 1:3-5, 18-21

3 Blessed be the God and Father of our Lord Jesus Christ! According to his great mercy, he has caused us to be born again to a living hope through the resurrection of Jesus Christ from the dead, 4 to an inheritance that is imperishable, undefiled, and unfading, kept in heaven for you, 5 who by God's power are being guarded through faith for a salvation ready to be revealed in the last time.

18 knowing that you were ransomed from the futile ways inherited from your forefathers, not with perishable things such as silver or gold, 19 but with the precious blood of Christ, like that of a lamb without blemish or spot. 20 He was

foreknown before the foundation of the world but was made manifest in the last times for the sake of you ²¹ who through him are believers in God, who raised him from the dead and gave him glory, so that your faith and hope are in God.

Philippians 3:7-11

⁷ But whatever gain I had, I counted as loss for the sake of Christ. ⁸ Indeed, I count everything as loss because of the surpassing worth of knowing Christ Jesus my Lord. For his sake I have suffered the loss of all things and count them as rubbish, in order that I may gain Christ ⁹ and be found in him, not having a righteousness of my own that comes from the law, but that which comes through faith in Christ, the righteousness from God that depends on faith— ¹⁰ that I may know him and the power of his resurrection, and may share his sufferings, becoming like him in his death, ¹¹ that by any means possible I may attain the resurrection from the dead.

How does this comfort you?

3. How does viewing Christ as our treasure change the way you view your life?

How will it change the way you view your day today?

Based on your Observation and Interpretation, how would YOU pray this prayer? Take some time to journal through or pray this psalm, based on your own thoughts and circumstances.

Praise

Psalm 19

Observation and Interpretation

Read Psalm 19 and consider the following questions.

¹The heavens declare the glory of God,
  and the sky above proclaims his handiwork.
² Day to day pours out speech,
  and night to night reveals knowledge.
³ There is no speech, nor are there words,
  whose voice is not heard.
⁴ Their voice goes out through all the earth,
  and their words to the end of the world.
In them he has set a tent for the sun,
⁵ which comes out like a bridegroom leaving his chamber,
  and, like a strong man, runs its course with joy.
⁶ Its rising is from the end of the heavens,
  and its circuit to the end of them,
  and there is nothing hidden from its heat.
⁷ The law of the Lord is perfect,
  reviving the soul;
the testimony of the Lord is sure,
  making wise the simple;
⁸ the precepts of the Lord are right,
  rejoicing the heart;
the commandment of the Lord is pure,

enlightening the eyes;
⁹ the fear of the Lord is clean,
  enduring forever;
the rules of the Lord are true,
  and righteous altogether.
¹⁰ More to be desired are they than gold,
  even much fine gold;
sweeter also than honey
  and drippings of the honeycomb.
¹¹ Moreover, by them is your servant warned;
  in keeping them there is great reward.
¹² Who can discern his errors?
  Declare me innocent from hidden faults.
¹³ Keep back your servant also from presumptuous sins;
  let them not have dominion over me!
Then I shall be blameless,
  and innocent of great transgression.
¹⁴ Let the words of my mouth and the meditation of my heart
  be acceptable in your sight,
  O Lord, my rock and my redeemer.

1. List some ways God declares His glory in verses 1-6.

2. In verses 7-11, we see God declares His glory through His word. In your own words, list some benefits of God's word as described in verses 7-11.

3. Read **John 1:1-4, 14-18**. How does God's revelation of Himself in His word point us to Jesus Christ?

[1]In the beginning was the Word, and the Word was with God, and the Word was God. [2]He was in the beginning with God. [3] All things were made through him, and without him was not any thing made that was made. [4]In him was life, and the life was the light of men. [5]The light shines in the darkness, and the darkness has not overcome it.

[14] And the Word became flesh and dwelt among us, and we have seen his glory, glory as of the only Son[a] from the Father, full of grace and truth. [15](John bore witness about him, and cried out, "This was he of whom I said, 'He who comes after me ranks before me, because he was before me.'") [16]For from his fullness we have all received, grace upon grace. [17]For the law was given through Moses; grace and truth came through Jesus Christ. [18]No one has ever seen God; the only God,[f] who is at the Father's side,[g] he has made him known.

3. In your own words, how does God's revealed glory inform the psalmist's response in verses 12-14?

Commentary and Teaching

Psalm 19 praises God for His revelation of Himself to us. Without His revelation, we would not know who He is. But He has chosen to reveal Himself so that we might know and love Him. Therefore, every part of His revelation is an act of mercy and grace. He is always speaking to us, and this psalm can help us respond to Him with praise.

Verse 1-6: David began with a list of the ways God makes Himself known to us. First, "The heavens declare the glory of God, and the sky above proclaims His handiwork." God speaks, or, "declares, and proclaims" His glory in the heavens. We can observe many things about the beauty of the heavens and how it speaks of the majesty and glory of God. Matthew Henry wrote, "From the excellency of the work we may easily infer the infinite perfection of its great Author.
From the brightness of the heavens we may collect that the Creator is light, their vastness of extent bespeaks his immensity; their height his transcendency and sovereignty, their influence upon this earth his dominion and providence, and universal beneficence: and all declare His mighty power…"(1706, Psalm 19). The NLT translates verse 2: "Day after day they continue to speak, night after night they make Him known." God faithfully, graciously, and continually speaks to us through the heavens.

In verses 3-6, David explained that the speech of the heavens is heard in every language, to every person, "their words to the end of the world." He shared how the sun joyfully gives heat to the whole earth: "nothing is hidden from its heat." The sun declares God's life-giving power to the earth. This also reveals His grace and heart toward His creation. In Matthew 5:44-45, Jesus further explained how God's glory in the skies reminds us of His grace. "But I say to you, love your enemies and pray for those who persecute you, so that you may be sons of your Father who is in heaven. For He makes His sun rise on the evil and the good and sends rain on the just and the unjust." We are to behold the heavens and be reminded of His grace and providence for all creation.

Verses 7-9: While the heavens speak of God's glory in unfathomable ways, verses 7-11 tell us how God persistently reveals His grace and pursues His people through His word. "Nature tells us about God's reality and power but not about His saving grace. Only the Bible can enlighten the spiritually blind..." (Keller, 2015, pg. 33). David transitioned and praised God for His glorious revelation of Himself in scripture.

The colons of the psalm here have a pattern: Colon A: Description of the word, Colon B: Benefit of the word to us. Ex: Verse 7, Colon A: The Law of the Lord is perfect Colon B: It revives our soul.

God's word is complete, and its purpose is to make us wise for salvation (2 Timothy 3:15). It's the word that "revives" and converts our souls, drawing us to Him (7a). The Message paraphrases verse 7b: "the signposts of God are clear and point out the right road." Scripture not only converts our souls but leads us on the right path to be followers of Christ, making us wise. Verse 8 tells us that His commands bring us joy. He has revealed Himself through instruction in the word that will lead us to enjoy Him. Psalm 16:11 tells us that in His presence is "fullness of joy, at [His] right hand are pleasures forevermore" (Psalm 16:11). His commandments "enlighten the eyes." Spurgeon expands and says, "… whether the eye be dim with sorrow or sin, the Scripture is a skillful oculist, and makes the eye clear and bright" (1993, Psalms, Vol 1., p. 68). God's word helps our vision to be clear and focused on the truth.

Verse 9 says, "The fear of the Lord is clean, enduring forever." This world will pass away (Revelation 21:1-2), but the legacy of Christ will last forever. As we respond to the fear of the Lord with obedience to His word, we can trust God will produce eternal treasure that will endure. Verse 9b adds that God's word is completely true and completely fair.

Verse 10: How should we experience God's word? We should value it as precious, more precious than gold. Matthew Henry expands: "Gold is of the earth, earthly; but grace is the image of the heavenly. Gold is only for the body and the concerns of time; but grace is for the soul and the concerns of eternity" (1706, Psalm 19). It is sweeter than honey. There is a special "sweetness" felt when we receive God's words to us; we should pray for this always. His words are meant to be treasured as an experience to "taste and see that the Lord is good" (Psalm 34:8).

Verses 11-13: As David responded to God's majesty and holiness, he realized his own imperfection. He reflected on the way God reveals Himself and became aware of God's ability to look into David's own heart. Here, David shows us how we should respond to God's word; we should let it search us and warn us. Only God knows our hearts, and His word is able to discern the thoughts and intentions of our hearts (Hebrews 4:12).

The NLT translates verse 13, "Keep your servant from deliberate sins, do not let them control me." Deliberate or presumptuous sins are done willfully. God has given us knowledge of Himself and His commands and boundaries. Think of a clear boundary that you know you are not to cross — a deliberate sin would be to acknowledge the boundary or commandment, understand it does not please the Lord, but deliberately cross over anyway. We "presume" we won't have consequences from these "presumptuous sins" even though we have been given God's revelation that plainly tells us where the boundaries are.

David was keenly aware, as we should be, that even though God has revealed Himself to us graciously through His creation and the word, he was still prone to ignore this knowledge and sin anyway. He asked God to help him to respond to His revelation correctly and obediently.

God can help us respond in worship and obedience as He changes our hearts through the Holy Spirit. As we become aware of God's holiness and our sin, we can put our hope in God's full revelation of Himself in Jesus Christ. John explains, "And the word became flesh and dwelt among us, and we have seen His glory, glory as of the only Son from the Father, full of grace and truth" (John 1:14). We can come to our Redeemer in our brokenness as we trust that when we confess our sins, He will reveal His grace to us as it was secured on the cross. A response to the revelation of His glory and grace is beautifully exemplified in the prayer at the end of the psalm. **"Let the words of my heart and the meditation of my heart be acceptable in your sight, O Lord, my Rock and my Redeemer"** (14).

Application and Reflection

1. Describe ways that the heavens inspire you to praise God.

How can singing and praying this psalm guide our worship when we behold the heavens?

2. Which benefit(s) of God's word stands out to you? Why?

3. How might this psalm inform our prayer life as we seek to know God through His word?

4. How can it inform the way our hearts should respond to God's revelation of Himself? (12-14)

5. How does God's revelation of Himself through Jesus strengthen and encourage your faith?

Based on your Observation and Interpretation, how would YOU pray this prayer? Take some time to journal through or pray this psalm, based on your own thoughts and circumstances.

Memory verse for this week: Psalm 1:5-6: Therefore the wicked will not stand in the judgment, nor sinners in the congregation of the righteous; for the LORD knows the way of the righteous, but the way of the wicked will perish.

Psalm 103

Observation and Interpretation

Read Psalm 103 and consider the following questions.

¹Bless the Lord, O my soul,
  and all that is within me,
  bless his holy name!
² Bless the Lord, O my soul,
  and forget not all his benefits,
³ who forgives all your iniquity,
  who heals all your diseases,
⁴ who redeems your life from the pit,
  who crowns you with steadfast love and mercy,
⁵ who satisfies you with good
  so that your youth is renewed like the eagle's.
⁶ The Lord works righteousness
  and justice for all who are oppressed.
⁷ He made known his ways to Moses,
  his acts to the people of Israel.
⁸ The Lord is merciful and gracious,
  slow to anger and abounding in steadfast love.
⁹ He will not always chide,
  nor will he keep his anger forever.
¹⁰ He does not deal with us according to our sins,
  nor repay us according to our iniquities.
¹¹ For as high as the heavens are above the earth,
  so great is his steadfast love toward those who fear him;
¹² as far as the east is from the west,
  so far does he remove our transgressions from us.
¹³ As a father shows compassion to his children,

so the Lord shows compassion to those who fear him.
¹⁴ For he knows our frame;[a]
  he remembers that we are dust.
¹⁵ As for man, his days are like grass;
  he flourishes like a flower of the field;
¹⁶ for the wind passes over it, and it is gone,
  and its place knows it no more.
¹⁷ But the steadfast love of the Lord is from everlasting to
everlasting on those who fear him,
  and his righteousness to children's children,
¹⁸ to those who keep his covenant
  and remember to do his commandments.
¹⁹ The Lord has established his throne in the heavens,
  and his kingdom rules over all.
²⁰ Bless the Lord, O you his angels,
  you mighty ones who do his word,
  obeying the voice of his word!
²¹ Bless the Lord, all his hosts,
  his ministers, who do his will!
²² Bless the Lord, all his works,
  in all places of his dominion.
Bless the Lord, O my soul!

1. Considering verse 1, what do you think David's purpose is
in writing this psalm?

2. From verses 2-22, list some ways David tells us to praise God regarding:

His salvation and the way He deals with our sin:

His limitlessness in contrast to our frailty and neediness:

His character:

Commentary and Teaching

David repeats the phrase "Bless the Lord" in this psalm. Some translations say, "Praise the Lord." "Jehovah is worthy to be praised by us in the highest style of adoration which is intended by the term 'Bless'" (Spurgeon, 1993, Vol. II, p. 71). David seems to overflow with blessing and affection for his God in Psalm 103. But when we look closely, we'll see that this hymn offers help for both times of plenty and times of need. We often turn to psalms of praise when we are joyful; that's certainly an appropriate time to use them. But there are times during trials that our deepest need is to turn our eyes upon Jesus in praise. It's in the weary circumstances, when we feel the frailest, that we need to remind ourselves of His tender care, His covering mercy, and His love that offers strength for endurance.

The seasons of our lives are always changing, but God is constant—and no matter what our circumstances are, our soul's greatest need is to praise God's unchanging attributes. In Psalm 103, David gave us words to help us talk to our souls and remind ourselves of His benefits and character.

Verse 1: "Bless the Lord, O my soul." David was talking to his soul and telling himself to praise God. He was pursuing a full and focused kind of praise as he wrote, "and all that is within me, bless His Holy name." Praising God while we are working, serving, or distracted will always happen when we have a full life. However, David shows us we should also be intentional about having time to praise God in this "all that is within me, bless His holy name" kind of way. It is healing and life-giving to have this kind of worship.

Verses 2-5: David reminded himself "not forget all His benefits." Forgetting God's goodness and grace toward us can lead us to despair. David listed some benefits of God's salvation in the next verses.

God pardons our sins and heals our diseases. David knew God was a redeemer and a healer who passes over our sins (2 Samuel 12:13). He had seen God's great forgiveness and restoring work in his life. On this side of the cross, we know that this "passing over" happens when our faith is in Jesus. Our sins are forgiven at the cross, and we are reconciled to God (Romans 5:1-3). Sometimes, God heals our physical diseases when we ask. This "healing of diseases" also has to do with our spiritual disease of sin. Because of our reconciliation to God, He can redeem our physical and spiritual diseases and use them to bring us closer to Him. Paul explained, "we rejoice in our sufferings, knowing that suffering produces endurance, endurance produces character, and character produces hope, and hope does not put us to shame, because God's love has been poured into our hearts through the Holy Spirit who has been given to us" Romans 5:4-5. God has taken care of our greatest need in saving us from sin, so even in the greatest physical and spiritual pain, we are not without hope of redemption; He uses it all for the healing and restoring of our souls.

He redeems our life from the pit. Apart from Him, we deserve the pit, or "death" as the NLT translates. But by grace in Christ, He redeems us from this and "crowns" us with honor we could never deserve. He uses our lives to demonstrate His love and compassion. He saves us "to the praise of His glorious grace, with which he has blessed us in the Beloved" (Ephesians 1:6).

As help for our weariness, "He satisfies [us] with good so that our youth is renewed like the eagles." He knows genuine goodness and therefore can fill our lives with helpful, good things that refresh us (James 1:17).

Verses 7-14: David praised God for His character. He is perfectly righteous and just, and He protects and executes judgements for those who are oppressed. God graciously makes Himself known to us, as He always has. He revealed himself to Moses and Israel as "gracious and compassionate, slow to anger and abounding in steadfast love" (Exodus 34:6). He is still this God for us today. The NLT translates verse 9: "He does not constantly accuse us," though we know He could. But He chooses not to deal with us according to what our sins deserve. He chooses to deal with us in grace and patience (10).

Why does He deal with us so gently and patiently? Because His love toward those who fear Him is higher and greater than we could ever imagine (11). So, in Christ, instead of giving us what our sins deserve, He removes them as far from us as the east is from the west (12). He is a compassionate Father toward us. And just like a good, compassionate Father, in parenting us, He is mindful of our frailty and weakness. He made us after all… "he knows our frame; he remembers that we are but dust" (13-14).

Verses 15-18: Here, David reflected further on how God meets our neediness and frailty with His eternal greatness and steadfast love. Our days are like grass- temporary. Like a flower, all it takes is the wind blowing over it, and it is no more. When it leaves, its surroundings soon forget its existence (16). Our lives and our influence are short and limited. But in contrast… "the steadfast love of the Lord is from everlasting to everlasting on those who fear Him. His righteousness to children's children (17). Matthew Henry says: "God's mercy is better than life, for it will out-live it." We can only love and commit to those around us for a short time, but God's faithfulness will endure forever to our children and their children who fear Him (Isaiah 40:8).

Verses 19-22: This God, the gracious and compassionate one who loves us and deals with us in mercy, who is gentle in our frailty, and eternal and infinite in steadfast love; He is the one on the throne. His sovereign control is over every detail of our lives; He even numbers the hairs on our heads (Luke 12:7) and He rules over all (19). As David finishes his reflection of God's goodness toward him, he realizes he is one with earth and heaven in praising God. "All His 'works' on earth and in heaven are already singing to God and one another, and he has taken up his unique part in the greatest chorus and symphony of all" (Keller, 2015, p. 256). David ended this psalm of praise by reminding the angels, the hosts, all His works, and his own soul to bless the Lord for who He is.

Application and Reflection

1. In verse 1, David talked to his soul, telling "all that is within him" to praise God. How often do you have focused time to praise God for who He is? What might this look like for you?

2. What attribute of God stands out to you in this psalm?

How can believing this about God inform the way you view your life?

How does it inform the way you view others?

3. What specific verses in this psalm inspire praise and comfort in your current circumstances?

Based on your Observation and Interpretation, how would YOU pray this prayer? Take some time to journal through or pray this psalm, based on your own thoughts and circumstances.

Acknowledgements

To my three girls, Charis, Elsie, and Abigail—the words of the Psalms have cared for my heart so much while I've cared for you. To my husband, Philip Lee, whose steady, constant belief in me lends me the bravery I need to take steps of faithfulness. Thank you to Annie Kate Saunders at Meliora Word for her helpful edits. To the women of Redemption Hill Church, who graciously held me up with such generous encouragement. And to Jesus, the King... truly anything for Him.

Bibliography

1. Taken from the ESV® Study Bible (The Holy Bible, English Standard Version®), copyright ©2008 by Crossway, a publishing ministry of Good News Publishers. Used by permission. All rights reserved.
2. Unless otherwise noted: Scripture quotations are from the ESV® Bible (The Holy Bible, English Standard Version®), copyright © 2001 by Crossway, a publishing ministry of Good News Publishers. Used by permission. All rights reserved.
3. Scripture quotations marked MSG are taken from *THE MESSAGE*, copyright © 1993, 2002, 2018 by Eugene H. Peterson. Used by permission of NavPress. All rights reserved. Represented by Tyndale House Publishers, a Division of Tyndale House Ministries.
4. Scripture quotations marked (NLT) are taken from the Holy Bible, New Living Translation, copyright ©1996, 2004, 2015 by Tyndale House Foundation. Used by permission of Tyndale House Publishers, a Division of Tyndale House Ministries, Carol Stream, Illinois 60188. All rights reserved.
5. Taken from *Psalms, The Crossway Classic Commentaries.* Vol. 1 and 2. by Spurgeon, C.H. Edited by Alister McGrath and J.I Packer. Copyright 1993. Used by permission of Crossway, a publishing ministry of Good News Publishers, Wheaton, Illinois 60187, www.crossway.org.
6. Henry, Matthew. (1706) Matthew Henry Commentary on the Whole Bible (Complete). Psalms. Available online at biblestudytools.com/commentaries/matthew-henry-complete/
7. Futato, Mark D. (2002) *Transformed by Praise: The Purpose and Message of the Psalms.* Phillipsburg, New Jersey. P&R Publishing Company.

8. Keller, Tim and Kathy. (2011) *The Meaning of Marraige, Facing the Complexities of Marriage with the Wisdom of God.* New York, New York. Penguin Random House LLC.
9. Keller, Tim and Kathy. (2015) *The Songs of Jesus, A Year of Daily Devotions in the Psalms.* New York, New York. Penguin Random House LLC.
10. Keller, Tim. (2012) *The Freedom of Self-forgetfulness.* Chorley, England: 10Publishing.
11. Longman, Tremper. (1988) *How to Read the Psalms.* Downers Grove, IL, InterVarsity Press.

www.ingramcontent.com/pod-product-compliance
Lightning Source LLC
Chambersburg PA
CBHW070440130626
46553CB00006B/2261